A Bible Study By
Melissa Spoelstra

Numbers

Learning Contentment in a Culture of More

Leader Guide

Abingdon Women / Nashville

Numbers
Learning Contentment in a Culture of More
Leader Guide

This book is printed on elemental chlorine-free paper.

ISBN 978-1-5018-0176-1

17 18 19 20 21 22 23 24 25 26—10 9 8 7 6 5 4 3 2 1
MANUFACTURED IN THE UNITED STATES OF AMERICA

CONTENTS

About the Author

Melissa Spoelstra is a popular women's conference speaker (including the Aspire Women's Events), Bible teacher, and writer who is madly in love with Jesus and passionate about studying God's Word and helping women of all ages seek Christ and know Him more intimately through serious Bible study. Having a degree in Bible theology, she enjoys teaching God's Word to the body of Christ and traveling to diverse groups and churches across the nation, even to Nairobi, Kenya, for a women's prayer conference. Melissa is the author of the Bible studies *First Corinthians: Living Love When We Disagree*, *Joseph: The Journey to Forgiveness*, *Jeremiah: Daring to Hope in an Unstable World*, and the parenting books *Total Family Makeover: 8 Steps to Making Disciples at Home* and *Total Christmas Makeover: 31 Devotions to Celebrate with Purpose*. She has published articles in *ParentLife*, *Women's Spectrum*, and *Just Between Us*, and writes a regular blog in which she shares her musings about what God is teaching her on any given day. She lives in Dublin, Ohio, with her pastor husband, Sean, and their four kids: Zach, Abby, Sara, and Rachel.

Follow Melissa:

🐦	Twitter	@MelSpoelstra
📷	Instagram	@Daring2Hope
f	Facebook	@AuthorMelissaSpoelstra
	Her blog	MelissaSpoelstra.com
		(check here also for event dates and booking information)

Introduction

I'm so glad you've decided to study *Numbers: Learning Contentment in a Culture of More*. Numbers may sound like an intimidating book of the Bible, but as we open its pages we soon discover how relevant it is to our lives today. The story of the wilderness wanderers is filled with such rich truths—especially when it comes to complaining and learning contentment. Like the Israelites who wandered in the wilderness, we've all experienced the ache inside for more. And we're all too familiar with our culture's many answers—suggesting that if we had a bigger house, a better friend, a faster phone, or more stuff, then we could be content. Yet even as we attain these things we find ourselves comparing and complaining without getting any closer to filling the ache inside.

But there's good news: the Bible tells us that we can *learn* to be content. The Apostle Paul said in Philippians 4:11, "I have learned how to be content with whatever I have." It takes intentionality as we learn to follow God's way, but the benefits are definitely worth it. So, know that I am cheering you on, dear leader, as you shepherd a group of ladies through this study to learn the art of contentment.

As we begin with the opening of the Israelite's story in Exodus and quickly move into the Book of Numbers, we'll see that God led the people of Israel out of slavery and provided for their needs in the wilderness with food, water, and guidance; yet still they grumbled. Though they came so close to the land God had promised them, they chose their own way instead of following God's instructions; and they were unable to enter the land for forty years because of their discontent and disobedience.

In the past I felt smug and condescending toward the wayward Israelites. After all, they wandered; they complained; they worshiped idols; they didn't respect their leaders; they doubted God. But I've discovered that I don't have to look farther than my own heart to find the very same tendencies. Like them, we often start off well but get tired along the way. Just as they did, we look at our circumstances through human eyes instead of keeping our eyes on the Provider. Often we overlook God's long-term blessings when confronted with daily discomfort. We too are so close to the life of faith that God longs to give us, but we keep taking the reins, trusting only what we can see and pouting about the obstacles in the way.

The New Testament tells us that these events in Numbers were written to warn us (1 Corinthians 10:6) so that we will not make the same mistakes and suffer the same consequences. (That alone is good reason for studying this book of the Bible!) God sent His only Son to die to set us free from the sin that leads to discontentment. So, rather than continuing in sin and missing our own promised land of peace and contentment in the life He has given us, by His grace we can learn to be content.

As you and your group journey with the Israelites during the next six weeks, you will tackle some very practical topics, learning how to

- recognize our own complaining
- be content while still being authentic about the difficulties of life
- accept short-term hardship in light of the greater good of God's ultimate deliverance
- understand the relationship between complaining and worry
- change our perspective from a posture of fear to a posture of faith
- respond to opposition, scary circumstances, and even blessings in ways that cultivate contentment
- realign with God's character and promises

Together you will discover that we arrive at God's promised land of peace and contentment only as we trust and obey our incredible God, who truly is more than enough. My prayer is that God's Word will be alive and active in your own heart as well as in the hearts of the women in your group. Whenever I lead or facilitate a group, the Lord seems to bring His truth home to me in a whole new way. So, I encourage you to let this message of contentment resonate in your heart first. Then you will be able to encourage, inspire, and challenge others to grow.

About the Participant Book

Before the first session, you will want to distribute copies of the participant book to the members of your group. Be sure to communicate that they are to complete the first week of readings *before* your first group session. For each week there are five readings or lessons that combine study of Scripture with personal reflection and application (boldface type indicates write-in-the-book questions and activities). Each lesson ends with a "Talk with God" prayer suggestion.

On average you will need about twenty to thirty minutes to complete each lesson. Completing these readings each week will prepare the women for the discussion and activities of the group session.

About This Leader Guide

As you gather each week with the members of your group, you will have the opportunity to watch a video, discuss and respond to what you're learning, and pray together. You will need access to a television and DVD player with working remotes.

Creating a warm and inviting atmosphere will help make the women feel welcome. Although optional, you might consider providing snacks for your first meeting and inviting group members to rotate in bringing refreshments each week.

This leader guide and the DVD will be your primary tools for leading your group on this journey to learn how to be content in a culture of more. Whether you choose to follow this guide step by step, modify its contents to meet your group's needs and preferences, or simply peruse it to find a few helpful tips, questions, and ideas, you will find in these pages some valuable tools for creating a successful group experience.

Getting Started: This is a list of strategies, options, and introductory information that will help you ensure good organization and communication. You will want to review this material and communicate relevant information to group members prior to your group session for Week 1, either via e-mail or in an introductory session (see more about this in Getting Started). Or you might consider adding fifteen to thirty minutes to your first session for reviewing some of these important housekeeping details. Whichever option you choose, be sure that group members have the opportunity to purchase books and complete the Week 1 readings before your session for Week 1.

Tips for Tackling Five Common Challenges: This section includes ideas for addressing recurring issues that come up when leading a group. Every leader knows that some group dynamics can be difficult to tackle. What will you do when one person dominates the discussion or cuts off another person who is speaking? All eyes will be on you to see how you will intervene or ignore these situations. Be sure to check out these five common challenges and ideas to help when you encounter them.

Basic Leader Helps: This list of basic leader tips will help you prepare for and lead each group session.

Session Outlines: Six adaptable outlines (one for each week) are provided to help guide your group time. Each begins with a "Leader Prep" section to assist with preparation.

Digging Deeper Articles Preview: At the end of the book, you'll find a condensed preview of one of the Digging Deeper articles that are available online at AbingdonWomen.com/NumbersDiggingDeeper. In these articles you will find second-level, concise information your group members do not have in their participant books, such as cultural insights, background information, commentary, and so forth. (You're encouraged to read the full articles online prior to your group session.) As you dialogue with God about leading each session, ask Him what parts of the corresponding Digging Deeper article He might want you to share with the group. This will give participants an opportunity to continue to learn new insights in your time together each week. Feel free to point your group members to the online articles in class or via e-mail, Facebook, Twitter, or other social media.

This study is designed for six weeks, with an optional introductory session. Or, if desired, you may choose to extend the study to eight or twelve weeks; see the options included in Getting Started. Again, whichever option you choose, be sure that group members have the opportunity to purchase participant books and complete the Week 1 readings before your session for Week 1.

Each of the session outlines in this book may be used for a 60-minute, 90-minute, or 120-minute session. The following formats are offered as templates that you may modify for your group:

60-Minute Format
Welcome/Fellowship (2 minutes)
All Play (3 minutes)
Digging Deeper Insights (4 minutes)
Prayer (1 minute)
Video (25 minutes)
Group Discussion (20 minutes)
Prayer Requests (5 minutes)

90-Minute Format
Welcome/Fellowship (5-10 minutes)
All Play (5 minutes)
Digging Deeper Insights (4 minutes)
Prayer (1 minute)
Video (25 minutes)
Group Discussion (25 minutes)
Optional Group Activity (5-10 minutes)
Prayer Requests (10 minutes)

120-Minute Format
Welcome/Fellowship (15-20 minutes)
All Play (5-10 minutes)
Digging Deeper Insights (4 minutes)
Prayer (1 minute)
Video (25 minutes)
Group Discussion (30 minutes)

Optional Group Activity (5-10 minutes)
Prayer Requests (15-20 minutes)

As you can see, the basic elements remain the same in each format: a welcome/ fellowship time, an "All Play" icebreaker question that everyone can answer, an opportunity to share insights with the group from the week's Digging Deeper article, a video segment, group discussion, and prayer time. The 90-minute and 120-minute options offer longer times for fellowship, discussion, and prayer plus an optional group activity. If you choose not to do the group activity, you may add that time to another element of the session, such as group discussion or prayer. (See Getting Started for notes about including food, planning for childcare, and other important organizational details.)

If you are new to leading Bible studies and/or would like to have a framework to follow, the session outlines will guide you. Note that more discussion questions have been provided than you may have time to include. Before the session, choose the questions you want to cover and put a check mark beside them. Page references are provided for those questions that relate to questions or activities in the participant book. For these questions, invite group members to turn in their participant books to the pages indicated.

If you are a seasoned group leader looking only for a few good questions or ideas, I encourage you to take what you want and leave the rest. After all, you know your group better than I do! Ask God to show you what areas to focus on from the week's homework and use my discussion outline as a template that you can revise.

Of course, the Holy Spirit knows the content of this study (His Word) and the women in your group better than anyone, so above all I encourage you to lead this study under the Holy Spirit's direction, allowing yourself the freedom to make any changes or adaptations that are helpful or desirable.

I'm excited that God has called you to lead a group of ladies through the Book of Numbers and the Israelites' wilderness journey. I am praying for you and believing God for the work He will do through your leadership. Now, let's get started!

Getting Started

Before your study begins, be sure to review the following introductory information that will help you ensure good organization and communication. You are encouraged to communicate relevant information such as the dates, times, and location for group meetings; when/where/how to purchase books; details regarding childcare and food; expectations and ground rules; and an overview of the study to group members during an introductory session or via e-mail before your session for Week 1.

1. Determine the length of your study. The basic study is designed for six weeks (plus an optional introductory session), but you also can plan for an eight- or twelve-week study.
    *   For a six-week study plus an introductory session, use the session guides in this book and the video segments on the DVD. Be sure to distribute books during the introductory session or prior to your session for Week 1.
    *   For an eight-week study, add both an introductory session and a closing celebration. In the introductory session, watch the introductory video message and spend time getting to know one another, presenting basic housekeeping information, and praying together (use the guide on pages 23-24). For a closing celebration, discuss what you have learned together in a special gathering that includes refreshments or perhaps a brunch, luncheon, or supper. A closing celebration provides an excellent opportunity for ongoing groups to invite friends and reach out to others who might be interested in joining the group for a future study.
    *   To allow more time for completing homework, extend the study to twelve weeks. This is especially helpful for groups with mothers of young children or women carrying a heavy work or ministry schedule. With this option, women have two weeks in which to complete each week of

homework in the participant book. In your group sessions, watch and discuss the video the first week; then review and discuss homework the next week. Some women find they are better able to complete assignments and digest what they are learning this way.

2. Determine the length of each group session (60, 90, or 120 minutes). See the format templates outlined on pages 8-9.

3. Decide ahead of time if you/your church will purchase participant books that group members can buy in advance during an introductory session or in advance of your first session, or if group members will buy their own books individually. If you expect each member to buy her own book, e-mail group members purchasing information (be sure to note the cost, including tax and shipping if applicable). Consider including online links as well. Be sure to allow enough time for participants to purchase books and complete the readings for Week 1 prior to your session for Week 1.

4. Create a group roster that includes each group member's name, e-mail, mailing address, and primary phone number. (Collect this information through registration, e-mail, or an introductory session.) Distribute copies of the roster to group members prior to or during your first session. A group roster enables group members to stay connected and contact one another freely as needed, such as when taking a meal or sending a card or note to someone who is sick, who has missed several group sessions, or who has had a baby or another significant life event. Group members may want to meet for coffee or lunch to follow up on things shared in the study as well. As women cry and laugh and share life together in a Bible study, their lives will be intertwined, even if for a short time.

5. Make decisions about childcare and food and communicate this information to group members in advance. Will childcare be offered, and will there be a cost associated with it? Will refreshments be served at your gatherings? (Note: If your group is meeting for sixty minutes, you will not have time for a formal fellowship time with refreshments. You might consider having refreshments set up early and inviting women to come a few minutes before the session officially begins.) If you choose to have food, the introductory meeting is a good time to pass around a sign-up sheet. In the Bible study group I lead, we like to eat, so we have three women sign up to bring food for each meeting. One brings fruit, another brings bread or muffins, and another brings an egg dish. Your group may want to keep it simple; just be mindful of food allergies and provide choices that will not exclude women.

6. Let group members know what to expect. Those who have never participated in a women's Bible study group may be intimidated, scared, or unsure of what to expect. Friends have told me that when they first came to Bible study, they were concerned they would be called on to pray out loud or expected to know everything in the Bible. Ease group members' concerns up front. Reassure the women that they will not be put on the spot and that they may choose to share as they are comfortable. Encourage participation while fostering a "safe" environment. Laying a few basic ground rules such as these can help you achieve this kind of environment:

   • *Confidentiality*. Communicate that anything shared in the group is not to be repeated outside of those present in the study. Women need to feel safe to be vulnerable and authentic.

   • *Sensitivity*. Talk about courtesy, which includes practices such as refraining from interrupting, monopolizing, or trying to "fix" shared problems. Women want to be heard, not told what to do, when they share an issue in their lives. If they have advice to share with an individual, ask them to speak with the person privately after study. When studying God's Word, some differences of opinion are bound to arise as to interpretation and/or application. This is a good place to sharpen one another and respectfully disagree so that you may grow and understand different viewpoints. Remind the women that it's OK to question and see things differently; however, they must be kind and sensitive to the feelings of others.

   • *Purpose*. The primary reason you are taking time out of your busy schedules to meet together is to study the Bible. Though your group will pray for, serve, and support one another, your primary focus is to study the Bible. You learn in community from one another as you draw near to God through His Word. Though you may want to plan a service or social activity during the course of your study, these times should be secondary to your study time together. If group members express a desire for the group to do more outreach, service, or socials, gently remind them of the primary reason you gather.

7. Before the study begins, provide a short preview of the study's content, summarizing highlights in an e-mail or introductory session. Whet the appetite for what is to come by sharing (or reading) parts of the introduction from the participant book. Consider sharing a personal story that relates to the study's theme. What has been happening in your life recently that has given you an opportunity to learn contentment?

As you are enthusiastic about getting into God's Word together, your members will catch your contagious desire to focus on growing in contentment even in a culture fixated on more.

8. If you are having an introductory session, show the introductory video and open the floor for women to share in response to the questions on page 24.

9. Read the Week 1 Digging Deeper article "The Names of God" at AbingdonWomen.com/NumbersDiggingDeeper (see pages 58-60 for a condensed preview) for more insight into various names used for God in the Old Testament. Share these insights in an introductory session or during the Digging Deeper Insights segment of your first session.

10. Be sure to communicate to participants that they are to read Week 1 in the participant book prior to your session for Week 1. Review the options for study found in the introduction to the participant book and encourage participants to choose the options they plan to complete and then share this information with someone in the group for accountability.

Tips for Tackling Five Common Challenges

Challenge #1: Preparation

Do you know that feeling when Bible study is in two days and you haven't even finished the homework, much less prepared for the group session? We've all been there. When I'm unprepared, I can sense the difference when I'm teaching Sunday school, leading VBS, or facilitating discussion in my women's Bible study group. I'm hurried, scattered, and less confident when I haven't dedicated the proper time for preparation. It doesn't take hours, but it does take commitment.

I check myself with a little acronym when I prepare to lead: S-S-S. Many years ago I was asked to lead a segment on teacher training for a group of VBS leaders. I remember asking the Lord, "What are the most important things to remember when we handle your Word to teach?" As I sat listening, He gave me this process of S-S-S that has stuck with me through the years. It looks like this:

S – Savior. Know your Savior. We must spend time talking, listening, and staying closely connected with Jesus in order to lead well. As we intentionally keep our walk with Him close and vibrant, we can then hear His voice about how to structure our lesson, what questions to ask, and which verses in His Word to focus on.

S – Story. Know your story. Though God has been gracious to me when I have winged it, I feel the most freedom with God's truth when I have prepared thoroughly. Try not to cram in multiple days of homework at one time. Let it sink into your soul by reading curiously and slowly. Go back to areas that especially strike you and allow God to use His Word in your heart and mind so that you can teach with authenticity. Women can tell when you are flying by the seat of your pants.

S – Students. Know your students. Who are these women God has given you to shepherd? Are they struggling with finances, relationships, or body image issues? Are they mature Christ-followers who need to be challenged to go deeper in their study of God's Word or seekers who need extra explanations about where the books of the Bible are located? Most likely, you will be teaching to a wide range of backgrounds as well as emotional and spiritual maturity levels, and you will need God's wisdom and guidance to inspire them.

Challenge #2: Group Dynamics

Have you experienced that uncomfortable feeling when you ask a discussion question and a long silence settles over the group? With your eyes begging someone to break the ice, you wonder if you should let the question linger or jump in with your own answer. Other problems with group dynamics surface when Silent Suzy never contributes to the conversation because Talking Tammy answers every question. What does a good leader do in these situations? While every group has a unique vibe, I have found these general concepts very helpful in facilitating discussion.

First of all, a good leader asks questions. Jesus was our greatest example. He definitely taught spiritual truths, but one of His most effective methods was asking questions. Proverbs 20:5 says, "Though good advice lies deep within the heart, / a person with understanding will draw it out." As leaders, we must be intentional askers and listeners. I try to gauge myself throughout the discussion by reflecting often on this simple question: "Am I doing all the talking?" When I find I am hearing my own voice too much, I make a point to ask and listen more. Even if waiting means a little silence hangs in the air, eventually someone will pipe up and share. Women learn from each other's insights and experiences; we rob them of others' comments when we monopolize as leaders.

Now what about Talking Tammy? She not only answers every question but also makes a comment after each woman shares something (often relating to one of her own experiences). Try one of these transitional statements:

- "Thanks Tammy, let's see if someone else has some insight as well."
- "Let's hear from someone who hasn't shared yet today."
- "Is there anyone who hasn't talked much today who would be willing to answer this question?"

The hope is that Talking Tammy will realize that she has had a lot of floor time. Sometimes Talking Tammy also struggles to "land the plane." She can't find a stopping place in her story. Help her out by jumping in when she takes a breath and make a summary statement for her. For example, "I hear you saying that you could relate to the Israelites' tendency to grumble and complain. Anyone else find the struggles of the wilderness wanderers resonating in a similar way?" Occasionally I have had to take someone aside in a loving way and address her amount of talking. Pray hard and be gentle, but address the issue. As a leader, you must keep in mind the good of the group as a whole.

I once had several ladies leave the group because they were so frustrated by the continual barrage of talking by one woman in particular. Some of her many comments were insensitive and offensive to others in the room. I don't like confrontation, so I didn't want to address it. However, God grew me as a leader to speak loving truth even when it hurts for the benefit of those we are called to shepherd.

Sometimes even more challenging than Talking Tammy is Silent Suzy. We must walk a fine line as leaders, not putting on the spot those women who are uncomfortable talking in front of others. I have scared women away by being too direct. So how do we get Silent Suzy to talk without singling her out? Here are some ideas:

- If she is new to the study, don't push her at all during the first few sessions. Let her feel safe and get comfortable. Never call on her to pray out loud or single her out with a pointed question. I once said, "I want to know what Suzy thinks about this." All eyes turned on her, and I'll never forget the tears welling in the corners of her eyes as she said she wasn't comfortable being called on. She didn't come back to the group after that incident. How I wish I could have taken those words back. I learned a valuable lesson from that Silent Suzy—don't push!

- Listen with recall as she answers the All Play question that everyone is asked to answer. Watch for an opportunity to talk about something she has shared with a follow-up question that doesn't pry.

- Take her out for coffee and get to know her. With time, she might warm up and begin to contribute to the discussion. Through a deepened relationship, you'll get a better read on whether you should encourage her to talk.

Challenge #3: Prayer Requests

How often do we run out of time when sharing prayer requests, leaving us no time to actually pray? How do you handle those women who aren't comfortable praying out loud? What if your group has fifteen to thirty women, and just listening to everyone's prayer request takes half an hour?

It's so important to take the time to hear what is going on in each other's lives and to pray for one another. Here are some creative ideas I have learned from others to help keep prayer time fresh:

- As women enter the room, direct them to take an index card or sticky note and write their prayer request on it. Then during prayer time, each woman can read her request aloud, already having thought through it, and pass it to the woman on her right for her to keep in her Bible as a reminder to pray for the request until they meet again.
- Ask someone to record all the prayer requests and e-mail them to the group each week.
- If you have a small group, use a one- or two-minute sand timer when you are short on time. (Look in your game closet for one of these.) Lightheartedly tell each woman that she has one or two minutes to share her request so that each woman can have a turn. (You might want to flip it over again if tears accompany the request.)
- If you have more than ten women, divide into two or three groups for prayer time. Assign a leader who will facilitate, keep the group on track, and follow up. Sometimes our prayer group has gone out for breakfast together or gathered in someone's home to watch the teaching video again.
- Have women pick one or two partners and split into small groups of two or three to share prayer requests and pray for each other.
- Have an open time of popcorn prayer. This means let women spontaneously pray one-sentence prayers as they feel led.
- After everyone shares requests, ask each woman to pray for the woman on her right. Clearly say that if anyone is uncomfortable praying out loud, she can pray silently and then squeeze the hand of the woman next to her.
- Another option is to close the group in prayer yourself or ask a few women you know are comfortable praying in front of others to pray for the requests mentioned. Remember that many women feel awkward praying in front of others. Provide encouragement by reminding the group that prayer is talking to God and that there is no right or wrong way to have a conversation with our Creator. But always be sensitive to others and affirm that they will not be looked down on if they don't like to pray out loud.

Making a change in your prayer time occasionally keeps it from becoming routine or boring. Talking with Jesus should be fresh and real. Taking an intentional, thoughtful approach to this important time of your study will add great value to your time together.

Challenge #4: Developing Leaders

Women's Bible study groups are a great avenue for fulfilling the 2-2-2 principle, which comes from 2 Timothy 2:2: "You have heard me teach things that have been confirmed by many reliable witnesses. Now teach these truths to other trustworthy people who will be able to pass them on to others." As a leader, God calls us to help raise up other leaders.

Is there a woman in your group who is capable of leading? How can you come alongside her and help equip her to be an even better leader? Wonderful women have invested in me through the 2-2-2 principle, even before I knew that term. As an apprentice, I watched them lead. They gave me opportunities to try leading without handing the full reins over to me. Then they coached and corrected me. I have since had the privilege of mentoring several apprentices in my Bible study group and watching them go on to lead their own groups. This is multiplying leaders and groups, and God loves it!

Here is the 2-2-2 principle as laid out by Dave and Jon Ferguson in their book *Exponential*.[1] (My notes are added within brackets.)

- I DO. You WATCH. We TALK.
- I DO. You HELP. We TALK. [Have your apprentice lead a prayer group or an activity or portion of the session.]
- You DO. I HELP. We TALK. [Ask your apprentice to lead one session with you assisting with facilitation alongside her.]
- You DO. I WATCH. We TALK. [Give your apprentice full ownership for leading a session and resist the urge to jump in and take over.]
- You DO. Someone else WATCHES. [As God leads over time, encourage your apprentice to start her own Bible study group.]

My mentor and I led a Bible study group together for years. As the group grew larger, we both sensed God leading us to multiply the group, forming two groups. It was painful as we missed studying and working with each other. However, God blessed and used both groups to reach more women. Then a woman in my group felt called to lead her own study. She worried that no one would come to her group. She asked many questions as we worked through the 2-2-2 principle. Her first group meeting included eighteen women who now, five years later, still love meeting together. I've seen pictures of them on Facebook enjoying special times together, and I praise God for all that He is doing.

From our one Bible study there are now over five groups of women that meet regularly to study God's Word. This kind of growth begins with commitment to share leadership, follow the 2-2-2 principle, and multiply so that more women can grow in their walk with Christ. Don't miss the opportunity to develop new leaders with intentionality as you model and encourage other women to use their gifts.

Challenge #5: Reaching Out

How do you welcome new women into the group? This is especially tough if yours is an ongoing group that has had the same women in it for years. Newcomers can feel like outsiders if it seems like everyone already knows the unspoken rules of the group. Also, what about those who are finding their way back to God? Are they welcome in the group? While the purpose of the group is primarily Bible study, I've seen the Great Commission of making disciples happen many times through women's groups that meet for Bible study. God's Word will do the transforming work in their lives through the Holy Spirit. We are called to reach out by investing and inviting. Here are some ways a leader can help create an open group:

- End each Bible study with a closing celebration brunch, encouraging the women to bring food and friends. Some ideas for this time together include:
  - Have an open time when women can share how God worked in their lives through the Bible study.
  - Have one woman in the group share her testimony of how she came to understand the gospel and how it has been transforming her life recently.
  - Bring in a speaker from outside the group to share a testimony.
  - Make it fun! We play a fun group game (such as Fishbowl, Pictionary, or Loaded Questions) and have a white elephant jewelry exchange at Christmas. Women who might think Bible study is a foreign concept can see that you are just a bunch of regular women in pursuit of a supernatural God.
- Leave an empty chair in the group and pray for God to show you someone who needs a group of women she can study the Bible alongside.
- Though the main purpose of the group is Bible study, consider doing a service project together that you can invite other women to participate in (schedules permitting). Our group has made personal care bags for the homeless and also adopted a family at Christmas, which included going shopping for the gifts and wrapping them together. Depending on

where God is leading your group, serving together can help put hands and feet to the truths you are learning.

- Socials outside of Bible study also provide an opportunity to invite friends as a nonthreatening transition. While the focus of your group is much more than social, planning an occasional social event can be a good way to forge deeper connections. Our Bible study group has gone bowling together, had a backyard barbecue, and planned a girls' night out at a local restaurant. These times together not only help women get to know one another better but also give them a great chance to invite friends. These same friends who attend a social might later try a Bible study session once they have made connections with some of the women in the group.

---

1. Dave and Jon Ferguson, *Exponential: How You and Your Friends Can Start a Missional Church Movement* (Grand Rapids, MI: Zondervan, 2010), 58, 63.

Basic Leader Helps

Preparing for the Sessions

- Check out your meeting space before each group session. Make sure the room is ready. Do you have enough chairs? Do you have the equipment and supplies you need? (See the list of materials needed in each session outline.)
- Pray for your group and each group member by name. Ask God to work in the life of every woman in your group.
- Read and complete the week's readings in the participant book, review the session outline in the leader guide, and read the Digging Deeper article for the week. Put a check mark beside the discussion questions you want to cover and make any notes in the margins that you want to share in your discussion time.

Leading the Sessions

- Personally greet each woman as she arrives. If desired, take attendance using your group roster. (This will assist you in identifying members who have missed several sessions so that you may contact them and let them know they were missed.)
- At the start of each session, ask the women to turn off or silence their cell phones.
- Always start on time. Honor the efforts of those who are on time.
- Encourage everyone to participate fully, but don't put anyone on the spot. Invite the women to share as they are comfortable. Be prepared to offer a personal example or answer if no one else responds at first.
- Facilitate but don't dominate. Remember that if you talk most of the time, group members may tend to listen passively rather than to engage personally.

- Try not to interrupt, judge, or minimize anyone's comments or input.
- Remember that you are not expected to be the expert or have all the answers. Acknowledge that all of you are on this journey together, with the Holy Spirit as your leader and guide. If issues or questions arise that you don't feel equipped to answer or handle, talk with the pastor or a staff member at your church.
- Encourage good discussion, but don't be timid about calling time on a particular question and moving ahead. Part of your responsibility is to keep the group on track. If you decide to spend extra time on a given question or activity, consider skipping or spending less time on another question or activity in order to stay on schedule.
- Try to end on time. If you are running over, give members the opportunity to leave if they need to. Then wrap up as quickly as you can.
- Be prepared for some women to want to hang out and talk at the end. If you need everyone to leave by a certain time, communicate this at the beginning of the session. If you are meeting in a church during regularly scheduled activities or have arranged for childcare, be sensitive to the agreed-upon ending time.
- Thank the women for coming, and let them know you're looking forward to seeing them next time.

Introductory Session

Note: The regular session outline has been modified for this optional introductory session, which is 60 minutes long.

Leader Prep

Digging Deeper

Read Digging Deeper Week 1, "The Names of God" (see pages 58-60 for a condensed preview; read the full article online at AbingdonWomen.com/NumbersDiggingDeeper). Note any interesting facts or insights that you would like to share with the group.

Materials Needed

- *Numbers* DVD and DVD player
- Stick-on nametags and markers (optional)
- Index cards (optional—Prayer Requests)
- Participant books to purchase or distribute

Session Outline

Note: Refer to the format templates on pages 8-9 for suggested time allotments.

Welcome

Offer a word of welcome to the group. If time allows and you choose to provide food, invite the women to enjoy refreshments and fellowship. (Groups meeting for sixty minutes may want to have a time for food and fellowship before the official start time.) Be sure to watch the clock and move to the All Play icebreaker at the appropriate time.

All Play

Ask each group member to complete this sentence: *I want to grow in contentment especially when it comes to* _____ *in my life.*

Distribute the participant books, and then have the group turn to the introduction (pages 5-8). Ask volunteers to read one paragraph each until you've read through the entire introduction. Point out the different options for study (page 8) and encourage each woman to prayerfully decide what level of study she would like to complete. Decide ahead of time whether you will ask all ladies in your study to take part in the Contentment Project or if you will offer it only to those who would like to participate. Decide whether you will all find your own contentment bracelets or if you would like to place a group order from www.mudlove.com/contentment. Ask: *Based on this introduction, what are you looking forward to about studying the Book of Numbers?*

Digging Deeper Insights

Share with the group the insights you gained from Digging Deeper Week 1, "The Names of God" (condensed preview on pages 58-60; full article at AbingdonPress. com/NumbersDiggingDeeper). Share one of God's names that especially stood out to you. Then say: *I don't know how much of a part the meanings of our names played in our parents' decisions to name us. However, God's names reveal His character. What name for God is meaningful to you in your current season of life?* If you choose, encourage group members to read the article online.

One option for developing leaders in your group is to invite up to six women to sign up to read one (or more) of the weekly Digging Deeper articles online, and then have each woman share the highlights of what she learned during the appropriate group session. Create a sign-up sheet that lists each week with the article name and the date of your group session. This will help you identify potential leaders as well as help pique the women's interest in "digging deeper."

Video

Offer a brief prayer and then play the Introductory Session video.

Discuss:

- What is something new you learned about the Book of Numbers, the story of the wilderness wanderers, or contentment?
- What is one thing you are looking forward to in this study?
- Why do you think having a balanced view of God's holiness and grace is important to learning contentment?
- How is the topic of contentment relevant to your life right now?

Prayer Requests

End by inviting group members to share prayer requests and pray for one another. Use index cards, popcorn prayer, or another prayer technique included in Tips for Tackling Five Common Challenges (pages 14-20) to lead this time with intentionality and sensitivity.

Week 1

CONTENT IN DELIVERANCE

Exodus 1–15

Leader Prep

Memory Verse

The LORD is my strength and my song;
*   he has given me victory.*
This is my God, and I will praise him—
*   my father's God, and I will exalt him!*
                    (Exodus 15:2)

Digging Deeper

If you did not have an introductory session, read Digging Deeper Week 1, "The Names of God," and note any interesting facts or insights that you would like to share with the group. (See pages 58-60 for a condensed preview; read the full article online at AbingdonWomen.com/NumbersDiggingDeeper.)

Materials Needed

- *Numbers* DVD and DVD player
- Stick-on nametags and markers (optional)
- Pens or pencils, index cards (Optional Group Activity)
- Index cards or sticky notes (optional—Scriptures and Prayer Requests)

Session Outline

Note: Refer to the format templates on pages 8-9 for suggested time allotments.

Welcome

Offer a word of welcome to the group. If time allows and you choose to provide food, invite the women to enjoy refreshments and fellowship. (Groups meeting for sixty minutes may want to have a time for food and fellowship before the official start time.) Be sure to watch the clock and move to the All Play icebreaker at the appropriate time.

All Play

Ask each group member to respond briefly to this prompt: *Think about a time when you moved from one place or town to another. What was challenging about that move?* (It could be any move—from childhood, young adult, or adult life.)

Read aloud or paraphrase:

> Moving offers opportunities for a fresh start where we can make friends, enjoy different scenery, and enjoy new adventures. At the same time, moves can be scary. The anxiety of the unknown can cause us to want to stay put. Even if our life is difficult where we are, at least it is familiar. Stepping out to move isn't easy, but it can bring freedom and adventure. The Israelites lived as slaves in Egypt but had a difficult time moving on, facing opposition from not only their captors but also their own discontent. They struggled with doing the hard work of trusting their leaders when life initially got harder. I believe we'll be able to identify with the need to learn contentment as we delve into the pages of their story of deliverance.

Digging Deeper Insights

If you did not have an introductory session, share the insights you gained from Digging Deeper Week 1, "The Names of God" (condensed preview on pages 58-60; full article at AbingdonWomen.com/NumbersDiggingDeeper). Share one of God's names that especially stood out to you. Then say: I *don't know how much the meaning of names played a part in our parents' decision to name us. However, God's names reveal His character. What name for God is meaningful to you in your current season of life?* If you choose, encourage group members to read the full article online.

Prayer

Before playing the video segment, ask God to prepare the group to receive His Word and hear His voice.

Video

Play the video for Week 1. Invite participants to complete the Video Viewer Guide for Week 1 in the participant book as they watch (page 38). (Answers are provided on page 61.)

Group Discussion

Video Discussion Questions

- Where do you tend to fix your gaze in the midst of the contentment thieves of life? What have you been "framing" or highlighting lately?
- How can you focus more on God and less on your obstacles or struggles?
- When deliverance seems slow or things get harder rather than easier, what helps you keep following God? How do you refocus your gaze on God?

Participant Book Discussion Questions

Note: Page references are provided for those questions that relate to questions or activities in the participant book.

Before you begin, invite volunteers to look up the following Scriptures and be prepared to read them aloud when called upon. You might want to write each of the Scripture references on a separate index card or sticky note that you can hand out.

Scriptures: Exodus 3:1-5; Proverbs 13:12; Exodus 4:29-31; Exodus 5:6-9; Exodus 6:6; Hebrews 9:13-15; Exodus 14:13-14; Exodus 15:1-18; Philippians 4:6

Day 1: *Accustomed to Slavery*

- If you could cry out to God to deliver you from one thing or circumstance right now, what would it be? (page 12)
- Read Exodus 3:1-5. How would you explain the difference between having "burning bush clarity" and wrestling to know God's instructions for next steps? What insights or experiences have been helpful to you when it comes to discerning God's will?
- Which of the examples of things that are God's will on page 14 did you star, indicating you would like to pursue it more wholeheartedly? What action step did you identify that you might take in this area? (page 15)
- What names for God did you list in the "Talk with God" prayer exercise? (page 15)

Day 2: *When Life Gets Harder*

- Read Proverbs 13:12. Tell about a time you found this verse to ring true in your life (whether in the past or currently).

- Describe a time when you felt that God wanted to use you to help others but you weren't excited about it. (page 17)
- Read Exodus 4:29-31 and Exodus 5:6-9. Can you think of a time when you were encouraged by God's promises but then soon found life getting harder rather than easier? (page 18)
- How does the illustration of complaining being like a rocking chair resonate in your life?

Day 3: The Price of Freedom

- What are one or two good things in your life that have come through difficulty? (page 22) Tell about these good things that resulted from a trial.
- What new insights did you gain from looking at the plagues in the three categories or groupings of irritation, destruction, and death?
- Read Exodus 6:6. What words did you write to describe God? (page 24) How does knowing that your God has such a powerful right arm encourage you right now?
- Read Hebrews 9:13-15. What has Christ done for us? (page 26) How do these verses encourage you in light of the sacrifice of Christ?

Day 4: When God Shows Up

- How can you relate to L. R. Knost's quotation about life being amazing, awful, and ordinary? (page 27)
- Read Exodus 14:13-14. How do these verses resonate in your life today? (page 28)
- Is there an area where God is asking you to quit talking about change so you can get moving? What is a first step you can take toward freedom in that area? (page 29)
- Read Exodus 15:1-18. Which words or phrases in this song of deliverance resonate with you? (page 30)

Day 5: New Challenges

- What are two or three things you have complained about this week? (page 33)
- The people of Israel were asking the question "What are we going to drink?" when they found the water at Marah was bitter (Exodus 15:24). How would you phrase a similar question to God regarding a need in your life right now? (page 34)
- Read Philippians 4:6. What instructions did Paul give the church regarding our worries? How did you fill in the blanks? (page 35)
- What insights that resonated with you did you include in the Weekly Wrap-up related to learning to be content in deliverance? (page 37)

Optional Group Activity (for a session longer than sixty minutes)

Have some fun while reviewing this week's lesson by playing Deliverance Charades. Divide the group into two teams, and write the following words on index cards: Egypt, Hail, Blood, Frogs, Cows, Darkness, Gnats, Death, Sea, Songs, Complaints, Water, Straw, Bricks. Feel free to add other words related to the study that you think would be entertaining to act out. Invite one team at a time to draw a card and act out a word, giving them a time limit of thirty seconds. For a fun variation, have each team choose one person to guess while everyone else acts.

Prayer Requests

Invite the group members to share prayer requests and pray for one another. Use index cards or sticky notes, popcorn prayer, or another prayer technique included in Tips for Tackling Five Common Challenges (pages 14-20) to lead this time with intentionality and sensitivity.

Week 2

CONTENT IN PREPARATION

Numbers 1–10

Leader Prep

Memory Verse

> May the LORD bless you
> and protect you.
> May the LORD smile on you
> and be gracious to you.
> May the LORD show you his favor
> and give you his peace.
>
> (Numbers 6:24-26)

Digging Deeper

Read Digging Deeper Week 2, "Substitutes," and note any interesting facts or insights that you would like to share with the group. (Read the article online at AbingdonWomen.com/NumbersDiggingDeeper.)

Materials Needed

- *Numbers* DVD and DVD player
- Stick-on nametags and markers (optional)

- Twenty different household items (or a photo of the items and means for projection), paper, pens or pencils (Optional Group Activity)
- Index cards or sticky notes (optional—Scriptures and Prayer Requests)

Session Outline

Note: Refer to the format templates on pages 8-9 for suggested time allotments.

Welcome

Offer a word of welcome to the group. If time allows and you choose to provide food, invite the women to enjoy refreshments and fellowship. (Groups meeting for sixty minutes may want to have a time for food and fellowship before the official start time.) Be sure to watch the clock and move to the All Play icebreaker at the appropriate time.

All Play

Ask each group member to respond briefly to this question: *What is something you have recently organized?*

Read aloud or paraphrase:

Whether it's a junk drawer, closet, room, work files, or vacation plans, getting organized helps us prepare. In this week's lesson, we saw the Lord instructing His people to count their resources, camp with a plan, and travel in an orderly fashion. Having a plan can have a big impact when it comes to contentment.

Digging Deeper Insights

Share the insights you gained from Digging Deeper Week 2, "Substitutes" (see AbingdonWomen.com/NumbersDiggingDeeper). Share any insights you gleaned from reading about the Levites substituting for the firstborn sons, who were required to be dedicated to the Lord. Then ask this question: How does seeing God's substitutionary actions in the Old Testament remind you of New Testament concepts regarding Christ? If you choose, encourage group members to read the full article online.

Prayer

Before playing the video segment, ask God to prepare the group to receive His Word and hear His voice.

Video

Play the video for Week 2. Invite participants to complete the Video Viewer Guide for Week 2 in the participant book as they watch (page 73). (Answers are provided on page 61.)

Group Discussion

Video Discussion Questions

- When and how does chaos steal contentment in your life? What is one way that organization, or preparation, helps increase your contentment?
- Are there people you may be under-appreciating in your life? If so, who are they?
- Where could a better plan eliminate some complaining in your life?
- What kind of organized plan do you need for continued spiritual growth?
- How do you need to plan for rest in your life right now?

Participant Book Discussion Questions

Note: Page references are provided for those questions that relate to questions or activities in the participant book.

Before you begin, invite volunteers to look up the following Scriptures and be prepared to read them aloud when called upon. You might want to write each of the Scripture references on a separate index card or sticky note that you can hand out.

Scriptures: 1 Corinthians 14:33; Romans 12:1; Numbers 6:1-8; Numbers 6:22-27; Numbers 8:1-4; 2 Samuel 22:29; Psalm 18:28; Matthew 5:14-16; John 8:12; 1 John 1:5

Day 1: *Taking Stock of Resources*

- Day 1 opens with a discussion of numbers and the name of the book we are studying. What are some numbers in your life that threaten to steal your contentment (scale, bank account, social media likes, and so on.)?
- Are there any battles or challenges looming in your life? If so, what are they? What resources has God made available to you to prepare for current and future battles? (pages 44-45)
- Who is someone God has given you as a resource in fighting your battles? How has the Lord used this person in your life to help you fight your battles? (page 45)
- We learned that comparing our callings can be a danger to contentment. How have you found that to be true in your life?

Day 2: *Getting Organized*

- What things have you started off well but struggled to finish? (page 47)
- Read 1 Corinthians 14:33. What are two areas where some organization and planning might bring more peace and contentment in your life? (page 50)
- Read Romans 12:1. What does God ask us to offer Him? (page 50) How can we live out this verse in daily life?

- The Tabernacle represented God's presence to the Israelites. How has God's presence comforted and encouraged you in the past?

Day 3: *Special Seasons*

- Read Numbers 6:1-8. What did you learn about the Nazirite vow from Day 3's lesson? Refer to the exercises on pages 55-56.
- How has an intentional time of fasting (from food or other things) brought benefit into your life?
- Is there a specific thing that God is calling you to consider taking a break from now? If so, what is it? (page 57)
- Knowing that perfection isn't expected when it comes to commitments, is there an area where you can "begin again" when it comes to spiritual rhythms? (page 58)

Day 4: *Blessings*

- What is a compliment someone has given you in the past that has stuck with you? (page 60)
- Read Numbers 6:22-27. What are the three blessings in these verses? Which blessing could you especially use in your life right now? (page 61)
- Is there someone the Lord brought to mind who needs some blessing from you? If so, who was it? If you reached out to this person during the week, share how that went. (page 62)
- When it comes to times of spiritual celebration, what practical changes could you make to better implement the practice of recounting God's blessings? (page 65)

Day 5: *Lights and Rest Stops*

- Read Numbers 8:1-4; 2 Samuel 22:29; Psalm 18:28; Matthew 5:14-16; John 8:12; and 1 John 1:5. To live in the light is to live intentionally. Which of these verses about light stood out to you? Refer to your summaries on page 67.
- What are some things that help you stay continually plugged in to God's Spirit as your source of power? (page 67)
- Where did the topic of rest hit home with you? What are some restful activities that replenish you when you feel depleted? (page 71)
- As you review the lesson this week, what stood out most to you?

Optional Group Activity (for a session longer than sixty minutes)

Collect twenty items and place them on a table where all the women in your group can see them, or you can take a picture of the items and project it on a screen (a good option for larger groups). Gather a variety of different objects: household items, office supplies, jewelry, food, silverware/dishes, small toys, game pieces, junk drawer items, and so forth. Then ask the women to divide into groups of four or five and spend three to five minutes working together to group the items into four categories by listing them on a piece of paper. They can discuss how to make connections based on things such as function, material, and location of use. The idea is to have fun, laugh, and come up with creative ways to organize the items.

When time is up, let the smaller groups share their ideas with the larger group (another three to five minutes). Discuss how being prepared and getting organized sometimes means coming up with creative solutions.

Prayer Requests

Invite the group members to share prayer requests and pray for one another. Use index cards or sticky notes, popcorn prayer, or another prayer technique included in Tips for Tackling Five Common Challenges (pages 14-20) to lead this time with intentionality and sensitivity.

Note: If you plan to do the Optional Group Activity next week, take time now to read over the activity so that you have time to acquire the water soluble paper and other materials needed.

Week 3

CONTENT IN UNCERTAINTY

Numbers 11–14

Leader Prep

Memory Verse

Do everything without complaining and arguing, so that no one can criticize you. Live clean, innocent lives as children of God, shining like bright lights in a world full of crooked and perverse people.

(Philippians 2:14-15)

Digging Deeper

Read Digging Deeper Week 3, "Meet Miriam," and note any interesting facts or insights that you would like to share with the group. (Read the article online at AbingdonWomen.com/NumbersDiggingDeeper.)

Materials Needed

- *Numbers* DVD and DVD player
- Stick-on nametags and markers (optional)
- Water soluble paper, which dissolves in water (check local office supply and craft stores or order online), pens, several large bowls of water, hand towels or paper towels (Optional Group Activity)
- Index cards or sticky notes (optional—Scriptures and Prayer Requests)

Session Outline

Note: Refer to the format templates on pages 8-9 for suggested time allotments.

Welcome

Offer a word of welcome to the group. If time allows and you choose to provide food, invite the women to enjoy refreshments and fellowship. (Groups meeting for sixty minutes may want to have a time for food and fellowship before the official start time.) Be sure to watch the clock and move to the All Play icebreaker at the appropriate time.

All Play

Ask each group member to respond briefly to this question: *What is an item you have more than enough of right now?*

Read aloud or paraphrase:

> Maybe you just stocked up on toilet paper or have several extra ink cartridges for your printer. Some of you may have more lipsticks, handbags, or books than you can count. Sometimes we stock up for emergencies—or just in case something happens. Fear of running out or not having all we need can threaten our ability to learn contentment. In these uncertain times, we must learn to trust that God is more than enough.

Digging Deeper Insights

Share the insights you gained from Digging Deeper Week 3, "Meet Miriam," (see AbingdonWomen.com/NumbersDiggingDeeper). Share how Miriam had great moments such as when she led the people in the Song of Deliverance after crossing the Red Sea. She also made some poor choices such as criticizing Moses, which led to a short bout with leprosy. She wasn't a superhero; she was a person loved by God but prone to sin just like you and me. Then ask this question: *Like Miriam, how have you had spiritual highs and lows in your own pursuit of following God?* If you choose, encourage group members to read the full article online.

Prayer

Before playing the video segment, ask God to prepare the group to receive His Word and hear His voice.

Video

Play the video for Week 3. Invite participants to complete the Video Viewer Guide for Week 3 in the participant book as they watch (page 104). (Answers are provided on page 61.)

Group Discussion

Video Discussion Questions

- Have you ever been given what you prayed for only to discover that it didn't satisfy? If so, talk briefly about that time.
- What can help to keep us from being critics? How can we shift from being critical to being part of the solution? Give an example from your own life, if possible.
- Which glasses do you tend to wear most often—the giant glasses, grasshopper glasses, or God glasses? What situation do you need to see right now from God's perspective so that you can enter into His promises?

Participant Book Discussion Questions

Note: Page references are provided for those questions that relate to questions or activities in the participant book.

Before you begin, invite volunteers to look up the following Scriptures and be prepared to read them aloud when called upon. You might want to write each of the Scripture references on a separate index card or sticky note that you can hand out.

Scriptures: Numbers 11:1-3; 1 Corinthians 10:10-11; Psalm 23; Numbers 11:18-20; Psalm 106:13-15; Numbers 12:1-3; Philippians 4:11-14; Numbers 13:25-33; Proverbs 1:29-33; Numbers 14:10-12; Exodus 34:6; Psalm 103:8; Micah 7:18

Day 1: *Contagious Complaining*

- Read Numbers 11:1-3 and 1 Corinthians 10:10-11. Does the Lord's serious tone regarding complaining surprise you considering how prevalent it is within the body of Christ today? Why or why not?
- Recall a time in your life when your complaints have caused others to complain as well (whether family, friends, coworkers, or others). (page 77)
- How is complaining to others different from complaining to the Lord? How would you describe the difference between sharing with authenticity and complaining?
- Read Psalm 23 aloud together. Which contentment definition or statement from Richard Swenson's book *Contentment: The Secret to a Lasting Calm* did you underline, and why? (page 79)

Day 2: *Too Much of a Good Thing*

- How would you complete this sentence? *I wish I had just a little more* _____. (page 81)

- Read Numbers 11:18-20. Can you describe a time when you got something you really wanted but it didn't live up to your expectations? (page 81)
- Read Psalm 106:13-15. The King James Version says that God "sent leanness into their soul." In what ways do you see the excess of our culture producing leanness in the soul?
- Share two good things the Lord has done in your past. (page 84)

Day 3: *Power Struggle*

- Read Numbers 12:1-3. What were the criticisms the two siblings made regarding Moses? (page 86) How have you seen comparison lead to envy in your own experiences?
- When it comes to criticism, what are some practical ways we can discern between stated reasons and the underlying real issues—without judging the motives of others?
- Read Philippians 4:11-14. Share the statement of intent to grow in contentment that you wrote on page 90.
- What are some practical ways you have learned contentment in your life? (page 91)

Day 4: *Giants and Grasshoppers*

- What challenges are you currently facing? What things seem to be standing in the way of you experiencing God's peace and contentment? (page 92)
- Read Numbers 13:25-33. What insights did you glean from this incident regarding the twelve spies?
- How have you seen pain come in unexpected places in your life? (page 93)
- As you consider the giant and grasshopper perspectives, which one are you struggling with more right now? What are some practical next steps you can take in order to renew your mind toward the God perspective?

Day 5: *Consequences*

- Read Proverbs 1:29-33. How do consequences (bitter fruit) keep us from repeating bad decisions?
- Read Numbers 14:10-12. Share a time when you were in a difficult situation and the Lord came to your rescue. (page 99)
- Read Exodus 34:6; Psalm 103:8; and Micah 7:18. How have you experienced God's grace even in the midst of consequences?
- What encouragement, conviction, and/or principles stood out most to you over the course of this week of study?

Optional Group Activity (for a session longer than sixty minutes)

Prepare ahead of time a few large bowls of water, and place them at the front of the room. Have some hand towels or paper towels for drying hands available as well. After giving the group instructions (see below), you might want to play some reflective music in the background as they prayerfully reflect and then wash their hands. ("No Longer Slaves," written by Brian Johnson, Joel Case, and Jonathan David Helser, is a great song related to our story and topic.)

- Pass out pens or pencils and small squares of water soluble paper (one or more to each woman).
- Invite the women to take some time to consider their current fears and uncertainties. Ask: *Are there any giant or grasshopper perspectives you need to hand over to the Lord? Is there an area in your life where you are scared you won't have enough (money, friends, support, work, or something else)?*
- Instruct them to write down any situations, burdens, anxieties, or fears they have been carrying that they want to release into God's hands.
- Say that God is the living water, and invite them to come up when they are ready and wash their hands with the paper(s) in their palms. Acknowledge that the papers will dissolve in the water.
- When all of the women have had a turn to release their uncertainties to the Lord, transition into a time of prayer.

Prayer Requests

Invite the group members to share prayer requests and pray for one another. Use index cards or sticky notes, popcorn prayer, or another prayer technique included in Tips for Tackling Five Common Challenges (pages 14-20) to lead this time with intentionality and sensitivity.

Week 4

CONTENT IN OBEDIENCE

Numbers 15–20

Leader Prep

Memory Verse

Be thankful in all circumstances, for this is God's will for you who belong to Christ Jesus.

(1 *Thessalonians* 5:18)

Digging Deeper

Read Digging Deeper Week 4, "Shadows" (see AbingdonWomen.com/Numbers DiggingDeeper), and note any interesting facts or insights that you would like to share with the group.

Materials Needed

- *Numbers* DVD and DVD player
- Stick-on nametags and markers (optional)
- Thank-you notes (at least three for each member) and pens (Optional Group Activity)
- Index cards or sticky notes (optional—Scriptures and Prayer Requests)

Session Outline

Note: Refer to the format templates on pages 8-9 for suggested time allotments.

Welcome

Offer a word of welcome to the group. If time allows and you choose to provide food, invite the women to enjoy refreshments and fellowship. (Groups meeting for sixty minutes may want to have a time for food and fellowship before the official start time.) Be sure to watch the clock and move to the All Play icebreaker at the appropriate time.

All Play

Ask each group member to respond briefly to this question: *What was one family rule in your house growing up?*

Read aloud or paraphrase:

Did your parents want to be sure lights were turned off when you left a room? Maybe they were strict about curfews or the buddy system. You may have similar or very different rules in your own family today. God gives His people instructions to be obeyed. He doesn't leave us to figure out how to live according to our logic, feelings, or experience. Because He made us and loves us, He tells us some things we should stay away from and others we should wholeheartedly pursue.

Digging Deeper Insights

Share the insights you gained from Digging Deeper Week 4, "Shadows" (see AbingdonWomen.com/NumbersDiggingDeeper). Share anything that stood out to you regarding how God interacted with His people in both the Old and New Testaments—same God, different covenants. Then ask this question: *How have you struggled to reconcile differences in the Old and New testaments?* If you choose, encourage group members to read the full article online.

Prayer

Before playing the video segment, ask God to prepare the group to receive His Word and hear His voice.

Video

Play the video for Week 4. Invite participants to complete the Video Viewer Guide for Week 4 in the participant book as they watch (pages 134). (Answers are provided on page 61.)

Group Discussion

Video Discussion Questions

- When do you find yourself falling into the comparison trap? How has gratitude been effective in helping you break free from this trap?
- What has the Lord called you to do in this season of life? Are you content with this calling? Why or why not? How can you work at it for God rather than for people?
- Are there any areas of partial or slow obedience in your life right now? Are you making excuses, doing things you shouldn't do, or neglecting to do what you know you should?

Participant Book Discussion Questions

Note: Page references are provided for those questions that relate to questions or activities in the participant book.

Before you begin, invite volunteers to look up the following Scriptures and be prepared to read them aloud when called upon. You might want to write each of the Scripture references on a separate index card or sticky note that you can hand out.

Scriptures: Genesis 12:2-3; Numbers 15:37-41; Deuteronomy 30:19-20; Numbers 19:1-9; Hebrews 9:11-15; Numbers 20:1-6

Day 1: Tangible Reminders

- J. R. R. Tolkien wrote, "Not all those who wander are lost."[1]
- Have you ever had a season that seemed like wandering, but looking back you can see God's hand in it? If so, tell briefly about that time.
- When has remembering the end result helped you push through the uncomfortable parts of a task? (page 108)
- Read Genesis 12:2-3. Whom did God say would be blessed through Abraham? Considering God's heart for all people, how can we share God's love with the nations, and how might answering that call help teach us contentment? (page 109)
- Read Numbers 15:37-41. Why did God say they needed a tangible reminder? What are some physical reminders that have helped or that could help you not to forget spiritual concepts—things that help you focus on and obey God's instructions? (page 112) If you are doing the contentment project, share how things are going with the bracelet.

Day 2: Significance

- What are some of the daily tasks that you perform in order to serve God and others? (page 115)

- What are three specific things you can be grateful for in relation to the responsibilities you have right now? (page 116)
- In what area of your life do you sense God calling you to serve faithfully for now, even though at times it is difficult, mundane, or unsatisfying? (page 118)
- What are some practical ways you can break free from comparison living?

Day 3: *Life and Death*

- What are some ways that disobedience to God's commands can lead to death physically, emotionally, spiritually, and relationally?
- What insights did you glean from the activity on pages 121-122 regarding the differences and similarities between the old and new covenants?
- Read Deuteronomy 30:19-20. How has following God led to life and peace for you personally? Share some of the examples you wrote on page 124.
- How do you see both God's holiness and His graciousness in today's verses?

Day 4: *Purified*

- What were some of the phrases, insights, or questions that stood out to you from your reading of Numbers 18? (page 125)
- Read Numbers 19:1-9. Do any of the characteristics of this red heifer scenario remind you of Christ? If so, which ones? (page 127)
- Read Hebrews 9:11-15. According to these verses, what has Christ accomplished for us? How is this good news for you personally?
- What questions or insights do you have regarding what we covered today in Numbers 18 and 19?

Day 5: *Arguing*

- What types of situations tend to bring out your argumentative nature?
- Read Numbers 20:1-6. What personal loss was Moses experiencing? What were the people blaming Moses for? How did Moses respond physically? (page 130) What reactions do *you* have regarding the people's complaints and Moses' response?
- Share with the group your own "grain, figs, grapes, and pomegranates" from the past that you have been complaining about. How have you been doing since releasing your desires to the Lord and praying for any true needs that you have right now? (page 131)
- Look over the week's lesson and find one or two insights that stood out to you.

Optional Group Activity (for a session longer than sixty minutes)

Our contentment clue word for this week is *grateful*. Bring a large pack of thank-you notes, and give each woman three note cards so that she may write a short note expressing gratitude to a few people. If time allows, let the women take turns sharing to whom they wrote and why.

Prayer Requests

Before sharing prayer requests, take time for a brief announcement if you will be doing the Optional Group Activity in your next group session. Ask each group member to bring a plastic two-liter soda bottle next week—along with an indoor starter plant if you do not plan to provide these. (You might send an e-mail reminder during the week.)

Invite the group members to share prayer requests and pray for one another. Use index cards or sticky notes, popcorn prayer, or another prayer technique included in Tips for Tackling Five Common Challenges (pages 14-20) to lead this time with intentionality and sensitivity.

---

1. J. R. R. Tolkien, *The Fellowship of the Ring* (London: Unwin Paperbacks, 1985), 324.

Week 5

CONTENT IN OPPOSITION

Numbers 21–26

Leader Prep

Memory Verse

Let's not get tired of doing what is good. At just the right time we will reap a harvest of blessing if we don't give up.

(Galatians 6:9)

Digging Deeper

Read Digging Deeper Week 5, "Context" (see AbingdonWomen.com/Numbers DiggingDeeper), and note any interesting facts or insights that you would like to share with the group.

Materials Needed

- *Numbers* DVD and DVD player
- Stick-on nametags and markers (optional)
- Small indoor starter plants and plastic two-liter soda bottles (either provide these or have the women bring them), scissors, potting soil, spade or scoop, cardstock, pens, tape or glue (Optional Group Activity)
- Index cards or sticky notes (optional—Scriptures and Prayer Requests)

Session Outline

Note: Refer to the format templates on pages 8-9 for suggested time allotments.

Welcome

Offer a word of welcome to the group. If time allows and you choose to provide food, invite the women to enjoy refreshments and fellowship. (Groups meeting for sixty minutes may want to have a time for food and fellowship before the official start time.) Be sure to watch the clock and move to the All Play icebreaker at the appropriate time.

All Play

Ask each group member to respond briefly to this question: *What is one household chore you would like to give up forever?*

Read aloud or paraphrase:

Sometimes we all just want to give up on things. Wouldn't it be fun to say we are forever done with cleaning, laundry, and answering e-mails? However, with these and many other chores, we have to stay the course. The good news is that the Lord has blessings for us on the other side.

Digging Deeper Insights

Share the insights you gained from Digging Deeper Week 5, "Context" (see AbingdonWomen.com/NumbersDiggingDeeper). Explain that context is important because it helps us understand Scripture in light of the culture and people represented in the original audience. Then ask this question: *How have you gleaned deeper meaning of a passage by reading the verses around it and understanding more about the human author, culture, and people involved?* If you choose, encourage group members to read the full article online.

Prayer

Before playing the video segment, ask God to prepare the group to receive His Word and hear His voice.

Video

Play the video for Week 5. Invite participants to complete the Video Viewer Guide for Week 5 in the participant book as they watch (page 163). (Answers are provided on page 61.)

Group Discussion

Video Discussion Questions

- How have you discovered in your own life that attitude is everything when it comes to fighting the battle of contentment? Give an example, if you can.
- How can impatience keep us from recognizing our blessings? Have you ever started to view God's gifts with disdain rather than with thankfulness? How did you recognize the shift, and what did you do about it?
- When has greed been a contentment killer for you?
- Are you striving to overcome any obstacles in your own strength right now? How might you win the battle by faith, not sweat?

Participant Book Discussion Questions

Note: Page references are provided for those questions that relate to questions or activities in the participant book.

Before you begin, invite volunteers to look up the following Scriptures and be prepared to read them aloud when called upon. You might want to write each of the Scripture references on a separate index card or sticky note that you can hand out.

Scriptures: Numbers 21:1-5; John 6:32-35; 1 Timothy 6:6-8; Numbers 23:13-26; Galatians 3:26-29; Revelation 2:14; 1 Corinthians 10:6-8; 1 Corinthians 10:12-13; Galatians 6:7-9

Day 1: *Occupied Territory*

- In what ways have you faced opposition or trials in your journey with the Lord? (page 137)
- Read Numbers 21:1-5. What two specific complaints did the Israelites make? When have you needed patience while waiting for something? (page 138) How have you seen impatience as a contentment thief in your own life?
- Read John 6:32-35. What is one way that God has satisfied your needs as the bread of life? Consider ways He has met your hunger for relationship, truth, wisdom, direction, or material necessities. (page 139)
- Review the sections on the bronze serpent and water. (pages 139-142) What connections did you discover between Christ and the bronze serpent? Between Christ and water?

Day 2: More Than Meets the Eye

- What are some practical ways Christ-followers can discern inappropriate spiritual practices? (page 144)
- In what ways do you see the pursuit of money, idolatry, or pleasure contributing to less contentment in our culture? (page 145)
- Read 1 Timothy 6:6-8. What is great wealth or gain? (page 145) How does this definition of contentment fly in the face of culture's definition?
- How does knowing that God can block the path with an angel and talk through a donkey impact any fears or worries you've been experiencing lately? (page 146)

Day 3: Persistent Opposition

- Read Numbers 23:13-26. What do you discover about God's nature in Balaam's second message or oracle (vv. 18-24), which is a blessing? (page 149)
- What kind of opposition has threatened to dam up the flow of God's blessings in your life lately? (page 149)
- Read Galatians 3:26-29. What makes someone a child of God? Who are the true children of Abraham? (page 151)
- What are some practical actions or habits that have helped you cling to the hope of God's blessings in the midst of opposition in your life? (page 151)

Day 4: Temptation

- What biblical truths stood out to you from studying Moab's seduction of Israel in Numbers 25?
- Read Revelation 2:14. What were the two ways that Balaam taught the people of Israel to sin? What, then, are the two sins of Balaam identified in this verse that we must avoid? (page 153)
- Read 1 Corinthians 10:6-8 and discuss how the wilderness story of Numbers 25 should impact us as believers. (page 155)
- Read 1 Corinthians 10:12-13. What does God say He will provide for us when we face temptation? (page 156) How has God provided *you* a way out in times of temptation?

Day 5: Regrouping

- How can you relate to the Israelites in having to adapt to change? What life changes did you check on page 158?

- As you contemplate your own changing circumstances, where might the Lord be calling you to learn from the past while looking forward rather than backward? (page 159)
- As you reflect on your life, when and how have you seen God redeem a bad situation and use it for good? (page 160)
- Read Galatians 6:7-9. How do these verses support God's interaction with Joshua and Caleb? How has the principle of sowing and reaping rung true in your life? As you reflect on these verses in relation to your own life, where is God calling you to "not become weary in doing good" (Galatians 6:9)? (page 161)

Optional Group Activity (for a session longer than sixty minutes)

I admit that I am not the best at keeping houseplants alive. One of the reasons for this is the need for perseverance. You have to consistently water and fertilize, and you must be sure the plant gets sunlight over the long haul. Also, you must know what your type of plant needs. Some need a lot of water and others only a little. The same goes for sunshine and fertilizer. I have started well with plants, but they always seem to die eventually on my watch. I believe this is because I am consistent at first but then get busy with life and neglect them. For a lesson in perseverance that will be an ongoing reminder of our study this week, put together some simple plants as a group. Either purchase the starters ahead of time or invite each woman to bring her own plant—along with a plastic two-liter soda bottle. Be sure to make this announcement a week in advance; you also might send a reminder e-mail. (You'll also need potting soil, a spade or scoop, scissors, cardstock, pens, and tape or glue.)

Here are some simple houseplant ideas:

- aloe
- jade
- rubber plant
- spider plant
- cactus
- African violet

Have the women cut the bottoms off the two-liter soda bottles, poke a few holes in the bottoms, fill them with potting soil, and plant their starters. Then have the women write the memory verse for the week on a piece of cardstock and attach it to the base with tape or glue for a reminder to persevere.

Prayer Requests

Invite the group members to share prayer requests and pray for one another. Use index cards or sticky notes, popcorn prayer, or another prayer technique included in Tips for Tackling Five Common Challenges (pages 14-20) to lead this time with intentionality and sensitivity.

Week 6

CONTENT IN BLESSINGS

Numbers 27–36

Leader Prep

Memory Verse

All praise to God, the Father of our Lord Jesus Christ, who has blessed us with every spiritual blessing in the heavenly realms because we are united with Christ.

(*Ephesians* 1:3)

Digging Deeper

Read Digging Deeper Week 6, "The Special Vest" (see AbingdonWomen.com /NumbersDiggingDeeper), and note any interesting facts or insights that you would like to share with the group.

Materials Needed

- *Numbers* DVD and DVD player
- Stick-on nametags and markers (optional)
- Whiteboard, posterboard, or chart paper and markers (Optional Group Activity)
- Index cards or sticky notes (optional—Scriptures and Prayer Requests)

Session Outline

Note: Refer to the format templates on pages 8-9 for suggested time allotments.

Welcome

Offer a word of welcome to the group. If time allows and you choose to provide food, invite the women to enjoy refreshments and fellowship. (Groups meeting for sixty minutes may want to have a time for food and fellowship before the official start time.) Be sure to watch the clock and move to the All Play icebreaker at the appropriate time.

All Play

Ask each group member to fill in the blank: I *am blessed because* _____. Read aloud or paraphrase:

God has richly blessed us. He has given us all that we need for life and godliness. He didn't even withhold His Son out of His great love for us. We must remember to count and share these blessings rather than hoard or manage them.

Digging Deeper Insights

Share the insights you gained from Digging Deeper Week 6, "The Special Vest" (see AbingdonWomen.com/NumbersDiggingDeeper). Share any insights you gleaned from reading about the Urim and the Thummim in this article. Then ask this question: *What are some ways the Lord has directed you through Scripture, the Holy Spirit, and the sense He has given you?* If you choose, encourage group members to read the full article online.

Prayer

Before playing the video segment, ask God to prepare the group to receive His Word and hear His voice.

Video

Play the video for Week 6. Invite participants to complete the Video Viewer Guide for Week 6 in the participant book as they watch (pages 196-197). (Answers are provided on page 61.)

Group Discussion

Video Discussion Questions

- What is the difference between managing our blessings and sharing them?
- When has sharing a blessing brought you joy?

- Why is it important to be intentional in remembering what God has done? What are some ways we can do this?
- Who is the Lord calling you to fight for? What can you do?

Participant Book Discussion Questions

Note: Page references are provided for those questions that relate to questions or activities in the participant book.

Before you begin, invite volunteers to look up the following Scriptures and be prepared to read them aloud when called upon. You might want to write each of the Scripture references on a separate index card or sticky note that you can hand out.

Scriptures: Numbers 27:1-11; Deuteronomy 3:23-26; Romans 12:1-2; Ecclesiastes 5:2; Matthew 5:33-37; 1 Thessalonians 4:7; Acts 7:30-45

Day 1: *Making an Appeal*

- If you could ask God for anything right now knowing that He would grant it, what would it be? (page 165)
- Read Numbers 27:1-11. How did Moses determine what to do in this case, and what was the Lord's response? Can you think of anything unfair or unjust in your world right now that you would like to appeal to the Lord to change? If so, what is it? (page 167)
- Read Deuteronomy 3:23-26. What was Moses' appeal and God's response in this case? Describe a time when you asked God for something and the answer seemed to be no. (page 170)
- What principles do you learn from the daughters of Zelophehad and Moses regarding making appeals to God and responding to His answers? (page 170)

Day 2: *Managing Our Blessings*

- What are some of the blessings the Lord has given you materially beyond food and clothing? (page 171)
- Read Romans 12:1-2. What is our sacrifice as believers? What are some practical ways we can offer our bodies and our lives as living sacrifices? (page 173)
- How do your spiritual holiday celebrations give you time to reflect on God and His blessings? In your times of celebration, how can you practically focus on God's intention for us to respond to His wonder with rest, relationship, and ritual? (page 175)
- What are some areas where you think people tend to manage their blessings rather than share them? (Think of any recent complaints you've heard—whether online or in person—that are actually tied

to blessings, such as having to drive kids around because God has provided the resources and opportunities for them to participate in music lessons, sports, and other activities.)

Day 3: *Fighting for Each Other*

- Read Ecclesiastes 5:2. How is the Holy Spirit nudging you to apply these principles of integrity in your life? Is there an area where you need to be true to your word or a situation where you need to use fewer words? (page 177)
- Read Matthew 5:33-37. Where or how is the Lord calling you to think about your "yes" and "no" when it comes to any decisions facing you? (page 178)
- Read 1 Thessalonians 4:7. How has access to inappropriate material through media and the Internet made the fight for purity more difficult today than it was in previous generations? As you listen to the Holy Spirit, who comes to mind who may need your help and support as they face their challenges? Can you think of a practical way you can encourage them? (page 181)

Day 4: *Remembering*

- What are some of the challenges you have encountered lately? (page 182)
- What lessons have you learned about God, yourself, and/or others in seasons that seemed like times of wandering? (page 184)
- How have the boundaries, rules, and instructions found in God's Word and the promptings of His Holy Spirit brought contentment into your life when you have followed them? (page 186)
- What are some "glimpses of grace" or spiritual blessings that stand out from your list or timeline on page 187 (even if they came through difficult seasons of life)?

Day 5: *Contentment Legacy*

- As you consider those who will come after you, what are some words that you hope will be associated with your legacy? (page 188)
- Read Acts 7:30-45. What stands out to you from these verses?
- What practical changes will you continue to implement after our study is over?
- Which week did you star as the one that most resonated with you? How do the themes of the week that you starred echo into your current circumstances? (pages 191-193)

Optional Group Activity (for a session longer than sixty minutes)

Numbers Jeopardy Review

Play this simple review game. Divide into two or three teams. Take turns choosing a category and point value. Remind the teams to phrase their "answers" in the form of a question.

Write the following categories and point values on a large whiteboard, posterboard, or chart paper:

Deliverance	Preparation	Uncertainty	Obedience	Opposition	Blessings
100	100	100	100	100	100
200	200	200	200	200	200
300	300	300	300	300	300
400	400	400	400	400	400
500	500	500	500	500	500

As a team selects a category and point value, find the corresponding answer below and read it aloud. Ask the team to phrase their response in the form of a question. If they give the correct question, award them the designated points (writing them on the board, poster, or paper) and invite them to choose another category and point value. If they do not answer correctly, deduct that point value from their total and give the next team a chance to answer. If that team answers correctly, they win the points and choose the next category and point value. Play continues in this manner until all of the categories and point values have been selected.

Deliverance

100 – This happened to the bush Moses saw. (What is burn?)

200 – Three of the ten plagues the Lord brought upon Egypt. (What are [name any three]: blood, frogs, gnats, flies, livestock, boils, hail, locusts, darkness, death of the firstborn?)

300 – How many Israelites wandered in the wilderness (What is over 1 million? or What is 2-3 million?)

400 – The names of Moses' two siblings. (What are Aaron and Miriam?)

500 – The video keyword for Week 1. (What is *focused*?)

Preparation

100 – What God said should be counted in chapter 1 of Numbers. (What is soldiers/ warriors/men able to go to war?)

200 – This was placed in the center of the Israelite camp. (What is the Tabernacle?)

300 – This vow required abstinence from wine and haircuts. (What is a Nazirite vow?)

400 – The material the lampstands in the Tabernacle were made from. (What is gold?)

500 – The video keyword for week 2. (What is *organized*?)

Uncertainty

100 – One of the things the people were complaining about in Numbers 11. (What is food/meat/manna?)

200 – God answered the people's cry for meat with this creature in Numbers 11. (What is quail?)

300 – The number of spies Moses sent to spy out the Promised Land. (What is twelve?)

400 – The names of the two spies who believed God about going into the land. (What are Joshua and Caleb?)

500 – The video keyword for week 3. (What is *enough*?)

Obedience

100 – This bloomed on Aaron's staff to confirm God's choice of him as a leader. (What is buds/blossoms/almonds?)

200 – This color of heifer was to be offered as a purification ritual for the people. (What is red?)

300 – The color of cord the people were to use to attach tassels to the edges of their garments in order to remember to obey in Numbers 15. (What is blue/violet?)

400 – This action kept Moses from getting to enter the Promised Land. (What is striking the rock twice instead of speaking to it?)

500 – The video keyword for week 4. (What is *grateful*?)

Opposition

100 – What Moses lifted up so that people could look at it and be healed from the plague of snakes the Lord sent. (What is the bronze serpent?)

200 – The animal that spoke to Balaam the soothsayer. (What is a donkey?)

300 – What Balaam spoke over the people of Israel instead of the curses King Balak asked him to pronounce. (What are blessings?)

400 – One of the two ways Balaam tempted the people of Israel when he couldn't curse them. (What is idolatry or immorality?)

500 – The video keyword for week 5. (What is *perseverance*?)

Blessings

100 – This is what the daughters of Zelophehad made an appeal concerning. (What is a claim of land so that their father's name would live on?)

200 – The name of Moses' successor. (What is Joshua?)

300 – What Moses reminded the people to continue presenting to the Lord once they reached the Promised Land. (What are offerings?)

400 – What two and half tribes requested to do. (What is settle on the other side of the Jordan River?)

500 – The video keyword for week 6. (What is *share*?)

Prayer Requests

Invite the group members to share prayer requests and pray for one another. Use index cards or sticky notes, popcorn prayer, or another prayer technique included in Tips for Tackling Five Common Challenges (pages 14-20) to lead this time with intentionality and sensitivity.

DIGGING DEEPER
WEEK 1 PREVIEW

THE NAMES OF GOD

See AbingdonPress.com/NumbersDiggingDeeper for the full article and other Digging Deeper articles.

In Old Testament times, the meaning of a name carried much greater weight than today. In a book about God's names, Kay Arthur writes, "In biblical times a name represented a person's character. God's name represents His character, His attributes, His nature. To know His name is to know Him."[1] Throughout the Book of Numbers, we encounter several of God's names that reveal His character.

Yahweh or Jehovah

Most often in the Book of Numbers we find God referred to as the Lord (see Numbers 1:1). In many translations, whenever the Lord appears in capital letters, it refers to the name Yahweh. The name Jehovah, which many people are familiar with, is actually based on a misunderstanding of how to pronounce the Hebrew word *Yahweh*. The Hebrew language is written with consonants on the main line of text, while the vowels are mostly represented as a series of marks above or below the consonants that help readers pronounce the words. The word *Yahweh* is written as YHWH, with vowel marks above and below. But because of a longstanding tradition that the name Yahweh was too sacred to pronounce, medieval Jewish scribes avoided using the true vowels for that name and substituted the vowels for the word *adonai*, which means "lord." Earlier Christian readers did not recognize the intention, and thought the proper pronunciation was "Yahovah," or Jehovah. Most biblical scholars believe that the word was originally pronounced Yahweh.[2]

Whether we use Yahweh or Jehovah isn't as important as understanding God's character behind His name, the Lord. *Strong's Concordance* cites the Hebrew word YHWH meaning, "the existing One." God is referred to as the Lord over 350 times in the Book of Numbers and over 6,000 times in all of Scripture.[3] This name reveals that He is self-existent; He was not created and is outside the limits of time. His character is revealed in this name as a God who is holy, set apart, unlike us. We can trust Him as the Lord who is greater and higher than we are. When trials, fears, or simply the doldrums of life are threatening to steal your contentment, you can run to Yahweh for safety.

We find many names of God that are compounded with Yahweh or Jehovah throughout the Old Testament, giving greater insight into the nature of the God we worship, such as Yahweh-Yireh (Jehovah Jireh), "The Lord will provide" (Genesis 22:14), and Yahweh-Nissi (Jehovah-Nissi), "The Lord is my banner" (Exodus 17:15).

El

Another name in the Book of Numbers that reveals God's character is El. This generic term for God that is used ten times throughout Numbers means, "God, god-like, mighty one."[4]

Elohim

The plural form of El is Elohim (or Elohiym), and this name is used twenty-three times in the Book of Numbers.[5] Elohim is the name of God used in the story of Creation. While scholars debate the reasoning for the plural, Elohim reveals God's majesty and power as ruler of the earth. It's interesting that in the creation story of Genesis 1, the verbs associated with Elohim are singular. This supports the idea that Elohim is a way of referring to the nature or character of the one God. Some other names of God that reveal His character are also compounds with the name El.

El Shaddai

El Shaddai is found in Numbers 24, verses 4 and 16. This name for God means the "all-sufficient One."[6] When the Spirit of God came upon Balaam the seer, he used the name El Shaddai in reference to the God who brought blessings on His people when others wanted God to curse them. God desires for us to see that He is all-sufficient to meet our needs.

El Elyon

El Elyon means the "Most High God,"[7] emphasizing God's strength and sovereignty above all creation—including all heavenly beings. It is also found in Numbers 24:16 when God is blessing His people through Balaam. God reveals that He is mighty and powerful to help us.

Adonai

Adonai, which means "my lord," [8] functions more as a title than a divine name. It is the title of reverence that Moses uses as he intercedes for the people when God wants to destroy them in Numbers 14:17. He humbly calls on Adonai, the Lord with total authority. Then he asks God to remember His unfailing love, forgiveness, and slowness to anger. As we approach God as Adonai, we must remember He has the power to do as He desires; but like Moses, we can ask for mercy and appeal to God's love and grace.

There are many other names in the Old Testament that reveal God's character. By studying God's names, we can know Him better; and as we know Him more, we can love and trust Him more. The more we know and embrace God's character, the more content we will be in focusing on Him rather than on our ever-changing circumstances.

---

1. Kay Arthur, *Lord, I Want to Know You: A Devotional Study on the Names of God* (Colorado Springs, CO: Waterbrook Press, 2000), 3.
2. For more on this subject, see "Is Jehovah God's True Name," Michael L. Brown, https://askdrbrown .org/library/jehovah-gods-true-name.
3. "Yehovah," http://www.biblestudytools.com/lexicons/hebrew/kjv/yehovah.html.
4. "El," http://www.biblestudytools.com/lexicons/hebrew/kjv/el.html.
5. "Elohim," http://www.biblestudytools.com/lexicons/hebrew/kjv/elohiym.html.
6. Arthur, 37.
7. "Elyown," http://www.biblestudytools.com/encyclopedias/isbe/god-names-of.html.
8. "Adonai," http://www.biblestudytools.com/encyclopedias/isbe/adonai.html.

VIDEO VIEWER GUIDE ANSWERS

Week 1

character / circumstances
harder
leaning
restful availability
do / find

Week 2

people
flexibility
preparation
rest

Week 3

seriousness
criticism
occupied

Week 4

help
comparison
disobedience

Week 5

Attitude
patience
look / Christ
enslave / control
Godliness / Contentment
strength

Week 6

pour out / manage
offerings
Remember
fight

Dig Deeper into Scripture and Find Inspiration with Other Bible Studies and Books by Melissa Spoelstra

First Corinthians: Living Love When We Disagree
Participant Workbook – ISBN: 9781501801686

Learn to show love when we disagree without compromising our convictions.

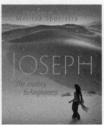

Joseph: The Journey to Forgiveness
Participant Workbook – ISBN: 9781426789106

Find freedom through forgiveness.

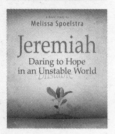

Jeremiah: Daring to Hope in an Unstable World
Participant Workbook – ISBN: 9781426788871

Learn to surrender to God's will and rest your hope in Him alone.

Total Family Makeover: 8 Practical Steps to Making Disciples at Home
Paperback Book ISBN: 9781501820656

Discover a practical approach to helping your children learn what it means to be followers of Jesus.

Total Christmas Makeover: 31 Devotions to Celebrate with Purpose
Paperback Book ISBN: 9781501848704

Connect your family more deeply with Christ during the holiday season.

DVD, leader guide, and kit also available for each six-week study.

Discover samples of her books and Bible studies at AbingdonWomen.com/MelissaSpoelstra.

Available wherever books are sold.

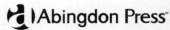

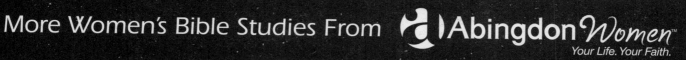

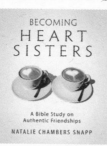

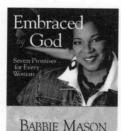